The

ULTIMATE
ROAD TRIP
JOURNAL
for Kids

The ULTIMATE
ROAD TRIP
JOURNAL
for Kids

INCLUDES 4 TRIPS!

Awesome Activities for Your Adventures

Kailan Carr

Illustration by Steve Mack

ROCKRIDGE
PRESS

To my favorite road trip companions—my husband
and two kids. Making memories with you on the
road and exploring new places is the best!

Series Designer: Merideth Harte
Interior and Cover Designer: Darren Samuel
Art Producer: Sara Feinstein
Editor: Jeanann Pannasch
Production Editor: Holland Baker
Production Manager: Jose Olivera

Illustration © 2021 Steve Mack. Author photo courtesy of Lando Lane Creative.

Paperback ISBN: 978-1-63878-153-0
R0

This
JOURNAL
belongs to:

Name:

Age:

Year:

TRIP № 1

It's time to hit the road! Show the route you'll be taking by drawing a line from the state you are starting in to the state you are headed to. If you are staying in the same state, circle the state you're in. You are going to have so much fun!

1

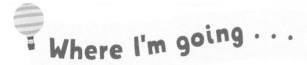

Where I'm going . . .

Are you ready to make some memories?
Record your trip plan here!

Date I'm leaving:

Where I'm going:

Place I'm leaving:

The trip will take:

hours/days/weeks (circle one)

I'm going with:

Free Drawing Space!

My Plans

The thing I'm most excited to do is

The site I can't wait to see or the thing I can't wait to do is

One thing I'd like to try is

One thing I'm curious about is

On the Road

The best part of the drive so far is

One thing I wouldn't want to happen again is

The weirdest thing I've seen out my window is

The coolest thing I've seen out my window is

LET'S BINGO-GO-GO!

Can you find all the items on the board? Look out for each item as you go, and if you see one, X it out. Fill in all the spaces for a total blackout, or complete a line across, up and down, or diagonally from corner to corner for Bingo!

BOREDOM
BANISHER!

Motorcycle	Horse trailer	School bus	Moving truck	18-wheeler truck
Delivery truck	Ambulance	Car with bumper sticker	Police car	A really dirty car
White van	Car with a dog in it	Traffic cone	Boat being towed	Motor home
Red truck	Blue car	Car with just two people	Four-lane road	Double yellow line
License plate from a state you don't live in	Tow truck	License plate with a Z in it	Bicycle	Car with the driver wearing a hat

MY VACATION SO FAR

Things I've Done So Far:
(check off all that apply)

- ❏ Went on a hike
- ❏ Played on the beach
- ❏ Looked for souvenirs
- ❏ Rode a roller coaster
- ❏ Saw a national landmark
- ❏ Walked through a museum
- ❏ Met new friends
- ❏ Visited family
- ❏ Other: _____

I think this trip is:
(check off all that apply)

- ❏ Fun
- ❏ Exciting
- ❏ Boring
- ❏ Exhausting
- ❏ Full of adventure
- ❏ Stressful
- ❏ Amazing
- ❏ Memorable

My favorite activity so far has been _____

_____.

I enjoyed this because _____

_____.

FUN WITH FOOD!

Trying new foods wherever you travel is part of the fun!

On this trip, I tried _____.

I thought it was _____.

Now draw the food in the blank space.

MEETING NEW PEOPLE

Road trips give you the opportunity to meet lots of new and interesting people! Write about some new friends you've met along the way.

I met _____ at _____ . They

were _____ .

I met _____ at _____ . They

were _____ .

I met _____ at _____ . They

were _____ .

Hello there!

Nice to meet you!

Nice car!

NEW EXPERIENCES ON THE ROAD ⇨ ➡ DATE:

Today, the weather was *(circle one):*

    ❑ Other_____

 An awesome new experience I had was

.

 One part that wasn't so great was

.

When I get home, I'm going to tell everyone about

.

Draw in the needle to show how awesome your day was.

9

DRAW WHAT YOU SEE

In the sunglasses, draw what you see looking out the window right now.

CITY LIFE

Can you find these big city words hidden among the letters in the grid? They can be vertical or horizontal. When you find one, circle it!

BOREDOM BANISHER!

A	T	C	H	I	M	S	E	A
P	H	O	E	N	I	X	R	C
A	D	A	L	L	A	S	N	H
R	E	N	O	N	M	D	E	I
Y	N	Z	L	K	I	B	O	C
T	V	A	T	L	A	N	T	A
S	E	A	T	T	L	E	R	G
X	R	B	O	S	T	O	N	O
N	E	W	Y	O	R	K	L	A

❑ Atlanta   ❑ Miami
❑ Boston   ❑ New York
❑ Chicago   ❑ Phoenix
❑ Dallas   ❑ Reno
❑ Denver   ❑ Seattle

Where Are You Going? Memory Game

This memory game is played with two or more players. Customize this game by using your destination, and then name the funny things you might be bringing with you. The first player starts by naming something they will bring that starts with the letter A. The next player has to repeat what the first player is bringing, and then add to it with a word that starts with the next letter of the alphabet.

For example:

The first player says: I'm going to Disney World and I'm bringing an <u>a</u>utograph book.

The next player says: I'm going to Disney World and I'm bringing an <u>a</u>utograph book and a <u>b</u>lanket.

The third player (or the first player if there are just two of you playing) says: I'm going to Disney World and I'm bringing an <u>a</u>utograph book, a <u>b</u>lanket, and a <u>c</u>ap.

The game continues until a player can't think of something to bring for their new letter, or can no longer remember everything you're bringing—or you finish the alphabet!

What I Heard Most

These phrases were on repeat in the car during our trip.

My   said

.

My   said

.

My   said

.

My   said

.

My   said

.

FIND THE ALPHABET

Look on billboards, license plates, buildings, road signs, or cars. Can you find the alphabet in order from A to Z? Color the letter in when you find it!

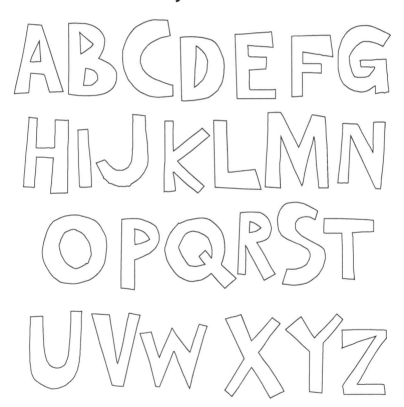

OH SAY, CAN YOU SEE?

Use the across and down clues to fill in the grid with the correct words. They are all sights you can see in the United States.

BOREDOM BANISHER!

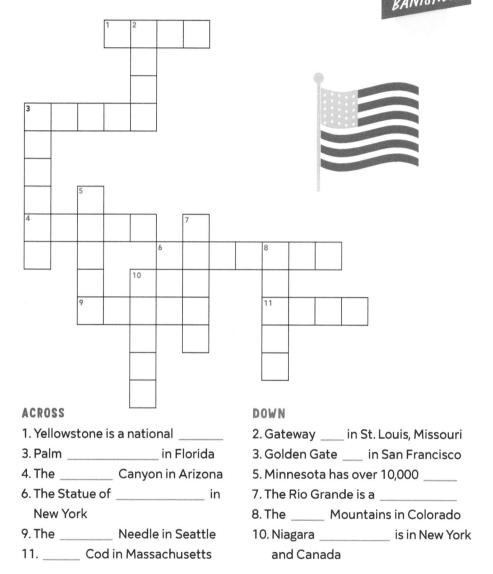

ACROSS

1. Yellowstone is a national _____
3. Palm _____ in Florida
4. The _____ Canyon in Arizona
6. The Statue of _____ in New York
9. The _____ Needle in Seattle
11. _____ Cod in Massachusetts

DOWN

2. Gateway ____ in St. Louis, Missouri
3. Golden Gate ____ in San Francisco
5. Minnesota has over 10,000 _____
7. The Rio Grande is a _____
8. The _____ Mountains in Colorado
10. Niagara _____ is in New York and Canada

15

ALMOST HOME!

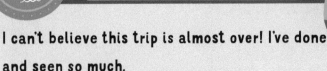

DATE:

I can't believe this trip is almost over! I've done and seen so much.

The most exciting thing I did was

_____

_____

_____.

The most beautiful sight I saw was

_____

_____.

One thing I learned was

_____

_____

_____.

TOP **5**

NEW OR COOL THINGS
I SAW ON THIS TRIP

17

*Take the time to write down any notes, memo
or other thoughts about your trip. You will lov
looking back at these later!*

TRIP № 2

WASHINGTON

MONTANA

NORTH
DAKOTA

OREGON

IDAHO

SOUTH
DAKOTA

WYOMING

NEBRASKA

NEVADA

CALIFORNIA

UTAH

COLORADO

KANSAS

OKLAHO

ARIZONA

NEW
MEXICO

TEXAS

It's time to hit the road! Show the route you'll be taking by drawing a line from the state you are starting in to the state you are headed to. If you are staying in the same state, circle the state you're in. You are going to have so much fun!

VERMONT

MAINE

NEW HAMPSHIRE

MASSACHUSETTS

RHODE ISLAND

CONNECTICUT

NEW JERSEY

DELAWARE

MARYLAND

WASHINGTON, D.C.

WISCONSIN

MICHIGAN

NEW YORK

PENNSYLVANIA

ILLINOIS

INDIANA

OHIO

WEST VIRGINIA

VIRGINIA

MISSOURI

KENTUCKY

NORTH CAROLINA

TENNESSEE

SOUTH CAROLINA

ARKANSAS

MISSISSIPPI

ALABAMA

GEORGIA

LOUISIANA

FLORIDA

Where I'm going . . .

Are you ready to make some memories?
Record your trip plan here!

Date I'm leaving:

Where I'm going:

Place I'm leaving:

The trip will take:

hours/days/weeks (circle one)

I'm going with:

Free Drawing Space!

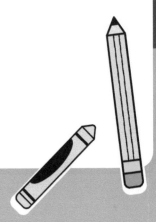

My Plans

The thing I'm most excited to do is

The site I can't wait to see or the thing I can't wait to do is

One thing I'd like to try is

One thing I'm curious about is

On the Road

The best part of the drive so far is

One thing I wouldn't want to happen again is

The weirdest thing I've seen out my window is

The coolest thing I've seen out my window is

LET'S BINGO-GO-GO!

Can you find all the items on the board? Look out for each item as you go, and if you see one, X it out. Fill in all the spaces for a total blackout, or complete a line across, up and down, or diagonally from corner to corner for Bingo!

BOREDOM BANISHER!

Cow		River		Tree
	Fence		Trash can	
Airplane in the sky	Billboard	Hay	Overpass	Barn
Cloud shape	Hotel	Mountain	Flowers	American flag
Solar panels	Power lines	Train	Tractor	Agriculture/ food growing
Mailbox	Building with at least 10 stories	Traffic light	Construction worker	Gas station

25

Would You Rather . . .

CIRCLE THE CHOICE YOU PREFER!

Would you rather ride on a motorcycle or in an 18-wheeler?

Would you rather go to an amusement park or a national park?

Would you rather get stuck in traffic or get lost?

Would you rather snack on chips or candy on a road trip?

Would you rather listen to podcasts or music on a road trip?

Would you rather be in a car with stinky feet or someone snoring?

Would you rather visit the Statue of Liberty or the Grand Canyon?

First Letter, Last Letter

This game requires two or more players. The first person says the name of a place, like California. The next person has to name a place that starts with the last letter in California. Let's say they choose Arkansas. The next person has to come up with a place that starts with "s," the last letter in Arkansas, and so on. You can change up the categories, too. For example, instead of places, you can use foods, items in a suitcase, animals, cities, and so on. Play until you can't think of any more words that match your theme.

MY VACATION SO FAR

So far, we've done all these things:
(check off all that apply)

- ❏ Swam
- ❏ Visited a museum
- ❏ Had 100 bathroom breaks
- ❏ Endlessly looked for parking
- ❏ Ate outside
- ❏ Used a map
- ❏ Hiked
- ❏ Bundled up

- ❏ Stayed out of the sun
- ❏ Took at least three group pictures
- ❏ Met somebody important or famous
- ❏ Jumped in a pile of leaves
- ❏ Saw wildlife
- ❏ Other: _____

My favorite activity so far has been _____

_____

_____ .

I enjoyed this because _____

_____

_____ .

NEW EXPERIENCES
ON THE ROAD ⇨ ➡ DATE:

Today, the weather was *(circle one):*

  ❏ Other

 An awesome new experience I had was

 One part that wasn't so great was

When I get home, I'm going to tell everyone
about

Draw in the needle to show how awesome your day was.

29

*Draw what you can see outside
your window right now.*

DATE:

MY TRAVEL STORY

Fill in the blanks to write your own tale. Ask your fellow travelers for suggestions based on the word prompts. The sillier, the better! Then read it aloud!

This trip was so _____ ! I can't believe we
fun or silly

traveled to _____ . The drive was _____
place   _description_

and took us _____ hours to get there. We saw
number

_____ on the way. I snacked on _____
thing   _food_

and listened to _____ . The best part was when
song

we _____ .
action

SPECIAL SOUVENIRS

Taking home a little reminder of your trip is special!

A souvenir I'm bringing home is _____ .

We got it at _____ , and I love it because _____

_____

_____ .

Draw a picture of your special souvenir or what you're looking for.

MOST LIKELY TO...

The person on this trip most likely to forget something is   .

The person on this trip most likely to make us laugh is

.

The person on this trip most likely to get lost is

.

The person on this trip most likely to need another snack is   .

The person on this trip most likely to need a bathroom stop is   .

ROAD TRIP AWARDS

The best snack I ate goes to .

The best song I heard goes to .

The best book I read goes to .

The best scenery I saw goes to .

The best animal I saw goes to .

WHAT IF...

If I forgot underpants, I would

If I saw someone famous on my trip, I would

If I could travel anywhere, I would go to

If I could pick any place in the world to live in, I would

choose

If we took a wrong turn and got lost, I would

DATE: _____

MY DAY AWAY!

I woke up at _____ .

The first thing I did was _____ .

One interesting thing I saw or did this morning was _____

_____ .

For lunch, I had _____ .

This afternoon, we _____

_____ .

Today was _____

because _____

_____ .

TOP 5

FAVORITE PLACES I VISITED OR THINGS I DID ON THIS TRIP

EXPRESS yourself

Take the time to write down any notes, memo or other thoughts about your trip. You will lov looking back at these later!

TRIP № 3

It's time to hit the road! Show the route you'll be taking by drawing a line from the state you are starting in to the state you are headed to. If you are staying in the same state, circle the state you're in. You are going to have so much fun!

Where I'm going . . .

Are you ready to make some memories?
Record your trip plan here!

Date I'm leaving:

Where I'm going:

Place I'm leaving:

The trip will take:

hours/days/weeks (circle one)

I'm going with:

Free Drawing Space!

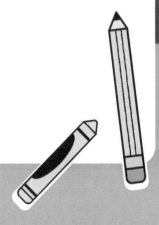

My Plans

The thing I'm most excited to do is

The site I can't wait to see or the thing I can't wait to do is

One thing I'd like to try is

One thing I'm curious about is

On the Road

The best part of the drive so far is

One thing I wouldn't want to happen again is

The weirdest thing I've seen out my window is

The coolest thing I've seen out my window is

LET'S BINGO-GO-GO!

Can you find all the items on the board? Look for these road signs as you go, and if you see one, X it out. Fill in all the spaces for a total blackout, or complete a line across, up and down, or diagonally from corner to corner for Bingo!

BOREDOM BANISHER!

Speed limit 55	One way	Adopt a highway	Call box	City limit sign
			CALL BOX	
Road construction	Speed limit 70	Black and white sign	Railroad	Deer crossing

Rest area	Traffic signal ahead	Keep right	Orange sign	Hospital (white H on blue sign)
				H
Merge	An arrow	No U-turn	Yield	Blue sign
Brown sign	Airport	Do not enter	Windy road	Gas

45

THOUGHTS IN MY HEAD

Driving time is the perfect time to think.

I am grateful for   .

I will try harder on   .

One goal I have is   .

I wonder if/why/about   .

NEW EXPERIENCES ON THE ROAD DATE:

Today, the weather was *(circle one):*

❏ Other_____

 An awesome new experience I had was

.

One part that wasn't so great was

.

When I get home, I'm going to tell everyone about

.

Draw in the needle to show how awesome your day was.

INTERVIEW THE DRIVER

Ask the driver these questions and mark their answers. Then draw a picture of the driver in the car.

Have you ever lived in a different state? ___Yes ___No

Have you ever had a flat tire? ___Yes ___No

Have you visited Yellowstone National Park? ___Yes ___No

Have you been to a theme park in Florida? ___Yes ___No

Have you driven more than eight hours in a day? ___Yes ___No

Have you been to the Statue of Liberty? ___Yes ___No

Have you swum in the Pacific Ocean? ___Yes ___No

Have you ever run out of gas? ___Yes ___No

Have you crossed our country's border in a car? ___Yes ___No

Are we there yet? ___Yes ___No

MY DAY AWAY!

DATE: _____

I woke up at _____ .

The first thing I did was _____ .

One interesting thing I saw or did this morning was

_____

_____

_____ .

For lunch, I had _____ .

This afternoon, we _____

_____

_____ .

The funniest thing that happened today was _____

_____

_____

_____ .

IN THE CAR

Use the across and down clues to fill in the grid with the correct words. They are all things you will find in the car.

ACROSS

3. Rearview _____
4. Windshield _____ is needed in rain
5. Music plays on the _____
7. Wear your seat _____
8. The glove _____ holds important papers
9. Fill up the _____ tank

DOWN

1. Says "beep beep"
2. The person steering the car
3. This helps you navigate
4. The steering _____ turns the car
6. You look out the _____
7. This stops the car

MY TRIP SO FAR

Things I've Done So Far:
(check off all that apply)

- ❏ Gone on a hike
- ❏ Played in the mud
- ❏ Found souvenirs
- ❏ Worn mittens
- ❏ Sat on a bus, train, or subway car
- ❏ Took a guided tour
- ❏ Made new friends
- ❏ Stepped on gum
- ❏ Visited family
- ❏ Other: _____ .

I think this trip is:
(check off all that apply)

- ❏ Fun
- ❏ Exciting
- ❏ Boring
- ❏ Exhausting
- ❏ Full of adventure
- ❏ Stressful
- ❏ Amazing
- ❏ Memorable

My favorite activity so far has been _____

_____.

I enjoyed this because _____

_____.

Make New Words

Rearrange the letters in ROAD TRIP to make new words—like PIT or DART. How many words can you make?

ROAD TRIP

License Plate Challenge

Color in any license plates you see during your trip.

ALABAMA	ALASKA	ARIZONA	ARKANSAS	CALIFORNIA
COLORADO	CONNECTICUT	DELAWARE	FLORIDA	GEORGIA
HAWAII	IDAHO	ILLINOIS	INDIANA	IOWA
KANSAS	KENTUCKY	LOUISIANA	MAINE	MARYLAND
MASSACHUSETTS	MICHIGAN	MINNESOTA	MISSISSIPPI	MISSOURI
MONTANA	NEBRASKA	NEVADA	NEW HAMPSHIRE	NEW JERSEY
NEW MEXICO	NEW YORK	NORTH CAROLINA	NORTH DAKOTA	OHIO
OKLAHOMA	OREGON	PENNSYLVANIA	RHODE ISLAND	SOUTH CAROLINA
SOUTH DAKOTA	TENNESSEE	TEXAS	UTAH	VERMONT
VIRGINIA	WASHINGTON	WEST VIRGINIA	WISCONSIN	WYOMING

WHAT A CRAZY SIGHT

Fill in the blanks to write your own tale. Ask your fellow travelers for suggestions based on the word prompts. The sillier, the better! Then read it aloud!

We went to explore _____ and we saw a
place

_____ . I was so _____ .
description   *feeling*

Then I started _____ .
action with -ing

_____ followed me to the _____ .
person   *place*

It was so _____ .
description

FUN WITH FOOD!

DATE:

Trying new foods wherever you travel is part of the fun!

On this trip, I tried _____.

I thought it was _____.

Now draw the food in the blank space.

PACIFIC OCEAN

I can't believe this trip is almost over! I've done and seen so much.

The most exciting thing I did was

.

The most beautiful sight I saw was

.

One thing I learned was

.

TOP **5** FUNNIEST MOMENTS ON THIS TRIP

EXPRESS yourself

Take the time to write down any notes, memories, or other thoughts about your trip. You will love looking back at these later!

TRIP № 4

WASHINGTON

MONTANA

NORTH DAKOTA

OREGON

IDAHO

SOUTH DAKOTA

WYOMING

NEBRASKA

NEVADA

UTAH

COLORADO

KANSAS

CALIFORNIA

ARIZONA

NEW MEXICO

OKLAH

TEXAS

It's time to hit the road! Show the route you're taking by drawing a line from the state you are starting in to the state you are headed to. If you are staying in the same state, circle the state you're in. You are going to have so much fun!

Where I'm going . . .

Are you ready to make some memories?
Record your trip plan here!

Date I'm leaving:

Where I'm going:

Place I'm leaving:

The trip will take:

hours/days/weeks (circle one)

I'm going with:

Free Drawing Space!

My Plans

The thing I'm most excited to do is

The site I can't wait to see or the thing I can't wait to do is

One thing I'd like to try is

One thing I'm curious about is

On the Road

The best part of the drive so far is

One thing I wouldn't want to happen again is

The weirdest thing I've seen out my window is

The coolest thing I've seen out my window is

LET'S BINGO-GO-GO!

Can you find all the words on the board? Look out for each word as you go, and if you see one, X it out. Fill in all the spaces for a total blackout, or complete a line across, up and down, or diagonally from corner to corner for Bingo!

BOREDOM BANISHER!

North	South	East	West	Left
Right	Mile	Exit	Caution	Rest
Number greater than 200	Number less than 20	Gas	Next	Speed
Turn	Number between 50 and 100	One	No	Road
Highway	City	Ahead	Lane	Traffic

MY VACATION SO FAR

So far, we've done all of these things:
(check off all that apply)

❏ Worn boots
❏ Visited people I never met before
❏ Had 100 bathroom breaks
❏ Endlessly looked for parking
❏ Ate outside
❏ Used a map
❏ Hiked
❏ Bundled up
❏ Stayed out of the sun
❏ Took at least two pictures without people in them

❏ Had to ask for directions
❏ Made souvenirs or crafts
❏ Saw wildlife
❏ Other: _____

My favorite activity so far has been _____

_____

_____ .

I enjoyed this because _____

_____

_____ .

NEW EXPERIENCES ON THE ROAD ⇨ → DATE:

Today, the weather was *(circle one):*

    ❏ Other

 An awesome new experience I had was

.

 One part that wasn't so great was

.

When I get home, I'm going to tell everyone about

.

TODAY ON THE

BLAH OKAY PRETTY GOOD AWESOME BEST DAY EVER

AWESOME-O-METER!

Draw in the needle to show how awesome your day was.

MAP OF YOUR SURROUNDINGS

Draw your car and what's around it from a bird's view above.

SEARCH FOR STATES

Can you find these state names hidden among the letters in the grid? They can be vertical or horizontal. When you find one, circle it!

T	G	E	O	I	O	T	N
N	E	V	A	D	A	E	A
M	O	H	I	O	I	X	K
A	R	I	Z	O	N	A	A
I	G	U	T	A	H	S	N
N	I	O	W	A	R	D	S
E	A	N	E	X	M	A	A
O	R	E	G	O	N	H	S

❏ Arizona
❏ Georgia
❏ Iowa
❏ Kansas
❏ Maine

❏ Nevada
❏ Ohio
❏ Oregon
❏ Texas
❏ Utah

WOULD YOU RATHER

CIRCLE THE CHOICE YOU PREFER!

Would you rather travel to the ocean or a forest?

Would you rather listen to silence or the same song on repeat?

Would you rather read or color in the car?

Would you rather travel to your favorite place again or explore new places?

Would you rather stay in a small town or a big city?

Would you rather forget socks or your toothbrush?

Would you rather see a bear or a moose in a national park?

EXPLORE YOUR SENSES

Right now, I see   .

Right now, I hear   .

Right now, I smell   .

Right now, I taste   .

Right now, I feel   .

Frozen in Time

In the state of _____, the price of gas is _____.

In the town of _____, the population is _____.

On the radio, a popular song is _____.

In the United States, the price of a stamp to mail a postcard is _____.

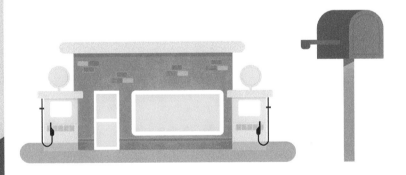

Postcard to a Friend

Write a note to your friend about your trip!

THINGS TO PACK

Use the across and down clues to fill in the grid with the correct words. They are all things you might pack for your trip.

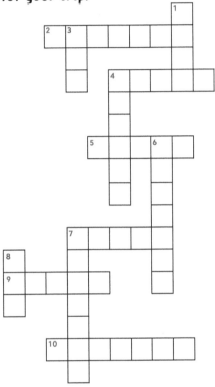

ACROSS

2. Use to wash your hair
4. Wear these with shoes
5. Don't forget your tooth _____
7. Wear this on your top half
9. A type of pants
10. Wear these if you need to see better

DOWN

1. Something to read
3. Wear on your head
4. Wear on your bottom half
6. For when it's cold
7. Shoes for warm weather
8. A short name for pajamas

SPECIAL SOUVENIRS

Taking home a little reminder of your trip is special!

A souvenir I'm bringing home is _____ .

We got it at _____ , and I love it because _____

_____

_____ .

Draw a picture of your special souvenir or what you're looking for.

MY DAY AWAY!

I woke up at _____ .

The first thing I did was _____ .

One interesting thing I saw or did this morning was

_____

_____

_____ .

For lunch, I had _____ .

This afternoon, we _____

_____

_____ .

Today was _____ because

_____

_____

_____ .

IXAT

TAXI

TOP 5
FAVORITE ACTIVITIES I'VE DONE ON THIS TRIP

EXPRESS
yourself

Take the time to write down any notes, memories, o
other thoughts about your trip. You will love lookin
back at these later!

Answer Key

Page 11

A	T	C	H	I	M	S	E	A
P	H	O	E	N	I	X	R	C
A	D	A	L	L	A	S	N	H
R	E	N	O	N	M	D	E	I
Y	N	Z	L	K	I	B	O	C
T	V	A	T	L	A	N	T	A
S	E	A	T	T	L	E	R	G
X	R	B	O	S	T	O	N	O
N	E	W	Y	O	R	K	L	A

Page 15

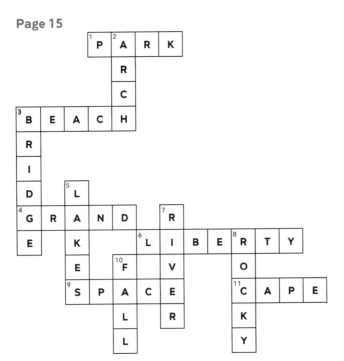

Crossword answers:

1 Across: PARK
2 Down: ARC
3 Across: BEACH
Down: BRIDGE
4 Across: GRAND
5 Down: LAKE / LL
6 Across: LIBERTY
7 Down: RIVER
8 Down: RTOKY...
9 Across: SPACE
10 Down: FVE...
11 Across: CAPE
Down: CKY

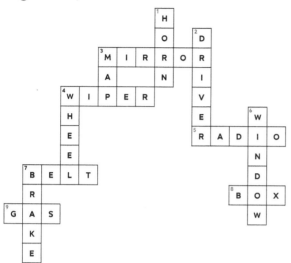

T	G	E	O	I	O	T	N
N	E	V	A	D	A	E	A
M	O	H	I	O	I	X	K
A	R	I	Z	O	N	A	A
I	G	U	T	A	H	S	N
N	I	O	W	A	R	D	S
E	A	N	E	X	M	A	A
O	R	E	G	O	N	H	S

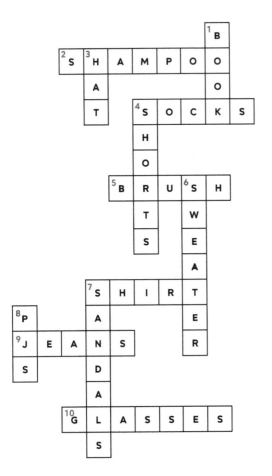

Acknowledgments

I'd like to thank Callisto Media for the opportunity to provide screen-free activities for kids! The timing was absolutely perfect. I was headed out on a three-week road trip through the northwestern United States with my family, which includes my seven- and nine-year-old, and I wrote this entire book during our driving hours! Thank you to my husband and kids for your inspiration and ideas. I love traveling with you, and the memories from this trip are priceless.

About the Author

 **KAILAN CARR** is a mom of two who is passionate about screen-free activities for little ones and big kids alike! She is an elementary educator who became a stay-at-home mom and then an entrepreneur. She started her business Quiet Book Queen and Crafts in Between (QuietBookQueen.com) to help parents and grandparents provide screen-free activities for little ones. This is her fourth book; her other titles include *Ocean Animals Preschool Activity Book*, *The Toddler's Science Activity Book*, and *Indoor Fun Preschool Activity Book*. She also loves road trips; her kiddos have traveled over 7,000 miles on summer trips keeping busy with activities like the ones in this book! Follow her at @quietbookqueen on Instagram and Facebook.